Beyond the Bars
One Woman's Journey to True Freedom

HEATHER A. COOK

Kingdom Builders Publications LLC

Beyond the Bars

ISBN:
Special Edition: 978-0-69250-699-8
Paperback: 978-0-69245-673-6
E-Book: 978-0-69245-674-3
Library of Congress Control Number 2015945775

Photography – LH "Just Pose" Photography
Cover Designer – LoMar Designs

Editors:
Jami Salters
Kingdom Builders Publication Staff
Wanda A Brown
Louise M Smith
Virginia Scott

Printed in USA
Go to our website: www.kingdombuilderspublications.com.

Beyond the Bars

Heather A. Cook

DEDICATION

I dedicate this book to my Savior, my Lord and my
Redeemer Jesus Christ, my Family, my beloved
children Jared, Logan, Darius, Kennedy and Ava-Grace
To my blood family and all my spiritual brothers and
sisters

CONTENTS

PROLOGUE

Everyone has a mask that covers a test that God wants to turn into a testimony.

How refreshing to see Heather take off her mask and be real with God and others. WOW! Her test has truly become her testimony to God!

> *And they overcame him by the blood of the Lamb and the word of*
> *their testimony; and they loved not their lives unto death.*
> *Revelation 12:11*

Heather will give readers the courage to live out loud and find their true identity in Jesus. In this book Heather encourages you to stop performing for a small crowd and just LIVE for the ONE. Heather's heart is on fire for God & you only need to be near her for a few minutes to see it burn.

Even though we are not flesh & blood, I am privileged to call her my sister. Heather challenges me!

> *As iron sharpens iron so a friend sharpens a friend.*
> *Proverbs 27:17*

We spend some of our favorite times; sharing how good God is over a cup of hot coffee....it's all about the relationship. So pour yourself a cup of coffee & sit with Heather as she tells you her story....

Lela Payne, Friend & Sister

PREFACE

We often hear people say "You don't know my story!" The truth is most people aren't willing to tell their REAL story. Maybe they fear rejection or the opinions of what others may think; compounded with shame and guilt. Who knows, but what I do know is most are NOT going to tell their real story!

In BEHIND THE BARS, you will get the raw, uncut, no candy coated, brutally honest account of life and the devastating effects of sin; what it does to us and those around us.
The road Heather traveled most of her life will bring tears to your eyes and pain to your heart.
I am so proud of my best friend Heather, whom I call my sister.

Heather and I met at the age of 12 in a runaway shelter. We were both very lost little girls with similar backgrounds; we were just looking for some love and acceptance.

Feeling like we didn't belong to anyone or anything, rebellion took root in our vulnerable years and our poor choices during adolescence took us both down the same broken road well into our adulthood. We were in an out of each other's lives even though we called each other friend, our relationship with each other was at best described as dysfunctional, manipulative and all about self-gratification. We would lie to each other, get high together, run the streets together and even steal from each other. We had no clue WHO we were, much less how to be a FRIEND.

We were grossly chained through the on slots of drug addiction. During our addictions, we were separated with very little communication with each other.

In 2010 God brought us back together again. Both of us had recently surrendered our lives to the Lordship of Jesus Christ. Little did we know how desperately we would need each other in this new walk of life but thank God, He knew!

This time our friendship is very different. Our friendship today has grown into a sister bond; one that I am truly thankful for! We hold each other accountable according to the Word of God, we are as *Proverbs 27:17ª* says, *iron sharpens iron* and as *Proverbs 17:17* teaches us, we try to be a *friend that loves at all times* even when we don't see eye to eye.

If you've ever met Heather I am sure you can agree she is some kind of special. With her super energetic personality, loving life attitude, big heart, beautiful smile, kind spirited; she definitely stands out!

There is no denying her love for the Lord as you watch her praise dancing or dancing with flags, running, shouting, or just lying in the middle of the floor not caring who's around.

The way she gets the kids involved during a worship service is indescribable... She's a worship warrior that will set something a fire inside of you; if you let it!

As you read her story, you will begin to understand her praise unto The Lord. Heather has experienced God's love. She knows who she is in Him. She has learned how to walk in forgiveness from those who have hurt her; most importantly she has forgiven herself. Heather has been set free! She is an Emerald of God's amazing grace, and every day she chooses to walk in all of that, in spite of how she may feel. TRUTH verses FEELINGS.

Jesus has already paid the ultimate price for our freedom *John 10:10*[b] *"Jesus died so that we may live and live more abundantly."* The question is are we living abundantly or are we like Heather once was, living behind bars?

As you read her book look at your own life.
What bars do you need to be free from? Bars of abuse, fear, depression, anger, bitterness, rejection, insecurity, loneliness, pride, rebellion, addiction? Allow Heather's transparency not to just inspire you or just encourage you but to help you on your own personal journey towards true freedom that can only be found in Jesus Christ.

John 8:36 says, "If the Son sets you free you'll be free indeed."

My prayer is that each person who comes across **Beyond the Bars** will experience God's amazing love,

His abounding grace and true freedom. As you read how Heather goes from death to life, understand that's the same way The Cross will take you from death to life.

Remember no matter what background you have come from, the enemy comes to steal, kill, and destroy. We each have our OWN story and the BATTLE is ALL the same, the enemy wants each one of us to walk in bondage!

The road to freedom is not always easy. Easy is going back to what we've always done. It will take determination and commitment. Leaving the familiar and walking sometimes crawling towards the unfamiliar can be a painstaking process. We must understand it is a process. Freedom does not happen overnight. The truth is we will always continue to experience new levels of freedom in Christ as we walk in direct relationship with Him!

~Freedom Awaits You...Trust the Process~
Jami Salters, Sister and friend for life

INTRODUCTION

LIFE AS I KNEW IT TO BE IS NOT LIFE AS I NOW KNOW IT.

This book is a biopic to introduce my life. I was born into a family that was already in captivity and didn't know how to show me my way out.

I know that I am not the only one who has wondered why I was the way I was. Surely it wasn't just me, this all had to come from somewhere. As I have had to go back several times to make peace with my past, I started to understand the root of where it all started. Because of that I have been able to let The Holy Spirit inspire me to share my story with you all. As you are reading my life story, know that it has not always been easy going back to get it right, but it sure has been worth it as The Lord, His comfort, peace and presence has been with me through it all.

I am NO longer a slave to fear, I AM A CHILD OF GOD!

CHOSEN BUT REJECTED

CHAPTER ONE

*A*s I began to ask The Holy Spirit to bring me back through the rolodex of my childhood, I remember when I was a little child I was already different from most little girls my age. Whereas the girl across the street liked to play with Barbie's and pink houses, I was busy playing in dirt, climbing in trees, looking for a ball & bat or some little boy to run around with. I was different and certainly stood out from the rest.

I have an older sister and younger brother, so that put me in the middle and labeled me as the Black sheep of the family. Well let's just say this is the first set of prison bars I sat behind. Negative labels are real and they are even harder to get rid of.

My father was a man who I used to see work hard all the time. He owned his own business as a mechanic in our back yard and that is where I discovered he called "home." My father was an outdoors man, so being the tomboy I was, I took interest in everything he did; hunting, fishing, in the woods, etc. The only thing wrong with this is it never taught me the fundamentals of life. What I took from the things I saw, heard and encountered was life is about having people around you to gather and drink, complain, and have a cussing match. I would hear things like; don't talk to me right now, go play, I'm busy. This is what I know now to be the start of my rejection and abandonment and made me feel unimportant.

I was at a place in my life where I felt if the only attention I could get was negative attention, then why not? I was different and everyone thought I was crazy so let me be just that.

You do become what you hear if you hear it enough and don't know how to counteract it. As a child I had dreams of what life should look like; such as excelling in academics, being the first female baseball player, or playing instruments. However the way my life was playing out then, I believed it just wasn't going to be so for me ever in life. Can you imagine the sound of the steel bars clanging? This was the reality of imprisonment of my mind; closed shut from truth and morality.

My family and their friends would gather together for drinking and I used that time to see what I could get away with. It's from stealing, smoking cigarettes, drinking unfinished bottles of beer, sneaking around the back of the house with boys in the neighborhood so they could feel me up. To looking at my dad's dirty magazines under the bathroom sink, and whatever else I felt I could get away with. Because of all the dysfunction in my house, it was easy to get away with things. However, my father had a very angry temper and when I got caught; there was no sparing the rod. He would take his frustrations out on us kids and our mother.

My mother had her own baggage and issues. She liked yelling and throwing things. I remember the time when we were getting ready for dinner. My father cozied up in his chair in the living room when my mother went on a tangent about something. My father chose not to follow up with his wife's madness. His quietness could have command the room to silence, but he just wanted to enjoy his rest. Suddenly, we saw an object fly like a fast ball in a major league game. A mason jar was fiercely in flight across the room; barely missing my father's head, and having a crash course with the wall as the canning jar went through it. This behavior was consistent toward my dad, my siblings and me; never a day without cursing, arguing and fighting. My mother seemed to always be unhappy. Now don't get me wrong, my family knew how to look "picture perfect." but we were so far from it.

My sister, who is the oldest, was the mascot and heroine of the family. Her goal was to make everything look perfect, but that was never the accomplishment. She wanted to save everyone all the time. She could never handle anything out of place or the ugliness of our family portrait. It must be perfect. She was considered the "*clean-up lady.*"

I remember looking up to my sister because it appeared she had favor with her peers, family, our mom and dad. She was a frilly girl liking girlie things such as girlie clothes, beauty pageants, having boyfriends, and she was a good student. My sister was greatly esteemed by others. I could never quite measure up. I just wasn't her. My family would always compare me to her by saying things like, "Well your sister did it!" or "Why can't you be more like your sister?" I guess that's why I never felt good enough. Once, I entered a beauty pageant to fit in, but felt so out of place. I won second place but even that was a problem because that didn't happen to my sister when she first started the pageant circuit. My second and final pageant was where I won the title of Ms. Ballantine/Chapin. This created more bars for me; no positive self-identity, living a lie in someone else's shadow.

My youngest sibling was a boy who was excused from a lot of misbehavior and bad choices. He and I would go at it hard. We physically and verbally fought all the time. Even though we shared a room together for a long time, we were constantly mean to each other. We gave each other scars and bruises that are still visible to this day. I don't remember ever seeing my brother chastised, scolded or punished for his bad behavior towards me. I remember the time he threw me off the bunk bed and I had to get stitches in my head, the time he threw something at me and I had to get stitches in my eye brow and even the time he pulled a knife on me. I tried to get it out of his hand but the price for that incident was freshly sliced thumb with a side order of stitches. Again and again, there was a role to play in being the brunt of my brother's anger issues and I seemed to be front and center to emotional and physical pain and scars. This is what I believe to be the beginning of the abuse I would endure from men later in life; another set of bars to sit behind.

It is fair to say that my family was one of much dysfunction and no direction. I spent a lot of time just trying to fit in and feel loved. I know now that they did love me, but at that time they were giving me all they had; they just didn't have much to give when it came to the *storge love. I now know they could only give what they had inside themselves to give; and if all they had was abusive language and behaviors, then that's what came out.

*Greek meaning Love of family; Parent/child, siblings, cousins, etc. - In a very close family, agape is felt as well)

Here we go again; another set of prison bars enclosed me; not knowing that real love could exist.

This introduction of my family gives a better understanding of why I struggled to find out who I was. There was NO UNCONDITIONAL LOVE or GUIDANCE from my family let alone spiritual guidance. There is neither LIFE going out nor life coming back in. As rejection set in, I looked for ways to be accepted.

I remember looking through my parent's room and discovered sex tapes, pictures of them, sex toys and magazines. I was about eight at this time and I became curious and wanted to watch the tapes. I would sneak them into the VCR while no one was in the house and I remember it making me feel good in some kind of way. I liked feeling that feeling.

It was self-gratifying and I thought I was feeling love, but rather it was an open door for evil and I had no idea the monstrosity of feelings that would turn my life events into explosive mind fields bringing forth death.

There was a family who lived across the street that had two boys and two girls. They were around the same ages as my siblings and me. We all used to play a lot together. One of the boys and I would touch each other. This to me was normal considering I was watching things that gave me good feelings and I liked to feel good. I just wanted to feel love and if this was it then I wanted more. I didn't want to feel unloved anymore. This was another hard slam of prison doors stealing time and innocence from my life.

Around this same time I had a great uncle that we used to go visit on a regular basis. There was something about him that was creepy and strange but on the other hand inviting. I was about ten years old and we were visiting for St. Patrick's Day. Everyone had been drinking and he just came over to me and started touching me. He would tell me that no one could know about us or I would never be able to visit him again. The thing is I never wanted to have this warped pleasure to cease because I enjoyed the way he made me feel and I wanted more. Although my innocence knew something wasn't quite right, I absolutely did not want anyone to take fun and love away and I never wanted to understand why it was wrong. So far all of this felt right because it's the only thing I found that made me feel like I mattered. I felt I was special to him and believed he had to have loved me to make me feel this way.

Man these bars are getting super thick around me. I am surrounded by thick metal and barbwire and don't even know it. Although my life was filled with lies and secrets; it was love to me. A monster was being created inside me and I didn't even know it.

Soon afterwards, my uncle committed suicide and I was devastated. The only person who ever showed me or gave me love was gone. I was confused and angry but was I in this emotional roller-coaster because he took himself away or further down was I angry because of what he did to me time and time again? These are the feelings of a lost little girl who is just looking to be loved by someone; anyone will do at this point.

I remember my parents wouldn't let me go to his funeral and that hurt me. There was a part of me I remember wanting to make sure he was really gone, but for what reason I was not sure of. I don't know if it was because I would miss him, or because I wanted him to be dead.

After the death and burial of my uncle, this is when I started having promiscuous encounters which made my life spiral out of control. I am now around eleven years old and the suicidal spirit of my dead uncle was trying to attach itself to me. I no longer wanted to live; I tried cutting myself several times but never could get it just right.

Rebellion became a close companion to me and I participated with that rebel spirit in any way I could. I became trouble in school by cheating on test, stealing from my teachers and peers, skipping class and fighting. The payoff for those behaviors was suspension and juvenile detention. I started running away from home every chance I got. I would go to school and just never come back home. I stayed at other people's homes until they would tell me I had to go home. I hated home because my family was a mess and so was I. Realizing that even the physical feeling of another human touching me was not enough anymore, I turned to drugs and alcohol. This is when my drinking and smoking pot came into play. I was still sexually active, now drugs were involved and this brought things to a whole new level of prison for me.

I was sentenced to juvenile detention for not going to school and for fighting, then I was placed in shelters for running away, and placed in alternative schools, one after another. I hated the humiliation of not getting it right therefore I attempted suicide again several times by cutting myself and taking pills. I was also in and out of mental hospitals more times like a broken revolving door, and the choice of cocktail to stabilize me was a host of psychiatric drugs. Given now the label of being a manic depressed child and another set of bars to sit behind.

A never ending story is what I call it. In the midst of all this, my family was still falling apart and I became the *fall girl* for blame. When I was 13, my mother threatened to leave my dad if he didn't find a solution for me. My behavior was so volatile and beyond reaching that everyone was on edge. Since I had a background of mental hospitals and psychiatric evaluations, and on psychiatric medication, my dad committed me to the state hospital and I spent the next six months of my life there. While in, I remember seeing some people who thought they could fly, others would talk to themselves as though they were sharing a conversation with a visible person. Then there were some people that would sit around in a strait jacket to protect themselves from themselves and others.

I have so many accounts of that dreadful place called the State Hospital. Like the time when I didn't take the prescribed medication, so I was put in solitary confinement in a padded cell where I stayed until I decided to adhere to the medication rule. It was very cold and lonely and the stench of urine and feces aligned the confined area walls.

What in the world is a child like me doing in a place like this and why are my parents the ones placing me here. Can't there be a better way? Certainly I am not classified with these kinds of people. No wonder I am in search of things, I have had no positive direction and I am now labeled yet again by man and society.

While I was put away, I was introduced to art therapy and felt like I made an inner connection. I understand it now... using colors helped my imagination and expressing me from the inside out got better. It felt as though I was gaining a sense of what was going on inside me. I believe God was speaking to me along this time and yet I still didn't know how to make a connection in the spirit because I didn't know there was a spirit.

Going back to when my mother said she would leave my dad if he didn't do something with me, well that's how I got to the state hospital. After being there a certain amount of time, I got to go home on weekends. This particular weekend while I was home on pass, my mother carried out her threat and left my dad anyway. Rejection and abandonment started hitting me hard. When my mother left my father, there were so many lies, deception and dysfunction. She said she would come to get us but would never show up; or when she did come, there would be fighting matches with my father that did not turn out well. My mother was in and out of abusive and dysfunctional relationships; one after another after she left my father. She eventually remarried a younger man, but he seemed to be different and very good to her. They relocated to Charleston, SC and the kids and I visited them a lot.

By this time I have had my oldest three kids. Reconciliation seemed to be in the making for my mother and me, but there was always hurt and bitterness in the attempt. Mother and her younger husband were blending a recipe for disaster. First, he started drinking more because he suffered from Post-

Traumatic Stress Disorder. That was probably triggered by an incident of a robbery that went wrong at the restaurant where he worked and was shot. They certainly had their issues to the point of another breakup. They did end up divorced after my mother took in my boys. I don't think that that was the final straw, but I believe it was just too much for the both of them to hold it together.

I remembered wanting someone to love me. Whomever I didn't care, please just someone. There were so many untapped feelings and emotions in me and I had no idea how to get rid of them. I was a little girl trapped in a woman's shell. Maya Angelo coined this phrase, "When someone shows you who they are, believe them the first time." That was the testimony of everyone around me. I was who people said I was and everyone told me I was trouble, so I believed their words. People told me I would never be any better, so I started to live it. Everyone told me I would never amount to anything, so I didn't. I took life as it was dealt to me and I didn't see a better way.

There were so many fears, hurts, rejections, and loss that I was in a dark place and I saw no way out but to die or numb all my pain. So I did just that from one place to the next; one abusive relationship to the next I dulled and numbed all the pain until I was mentally and emotionally dead. I went from one drug to the next;

anything, everything and anyone. This became my life's daily pattern and it seemed pretty normal.

My father remarried almost immediately. My step mother had two boys. Her oldest son was dating my sister when our parents met. When my dad was dating my sister's boyfriend's mother, it was most awkward when we'd all be together. They eventually broke up and my father stayed married to my stepmother until his passing. We were not the Brady Bunch. I spent a lot of time in Juvenile detention, a shelter or just gone while my step-brothers stayed in the house as a family. When I would make it home, I would take his car in the middle of the night while everyone was asleep and tried to return it before anyone would notice it missing. It didn't always work, so there wasn't much trust or relationship established.

My sister graduated and moved out from father's house. She had her own apartment and was managing a clothing store. I was sent off to Job Corps in Morganfield, KY. After being there for six months I got kicked out for alcohol, drugs and gang activity.

I was searching for love in all the wrong places. I got caught up in what I thought would be the key to finding love and happiness by being accepted into gang-life. My initiation into the gang life of the Crips through sexual activity and felt this was the answer to all my problems. I thought this was it; I have a new family. I was accepted with being under the eye, thumb and rule of someone who loved me only to find that the abuse I experienced was life threatening and taking life away from me more than it was producing. It was a life of fighting, beating and bloodshed. I believe when we all got in trouble and I got kicked out, it saved my life.

After getting back home, I didn't go to that lifestyle again, well at least to that degree and I'm thankful for that. When I returned, I had nowhere to go. My mom had no place of her own because she wasn't yet married, and my dad and stepmom were not letting me come there, so my sister agreed for me to come stay with her. I am 15 years old at this time and I've seen and experienced a lot. I met a guy named Travis. He was my sister's age and she introduced him to me just before I left for Job Corps. We started dating and he became my whole world. Travis, my sister and I would hang out regularly and Travis and I began to party quite frequently. Travis was a drug dealer and this is when I was introduced to cocaine. My whole world really began to change. This produced a whole new set of bars.

Cocaine was something I really began to love. I loved the way it made me feel, how it kept me up, how it helped me talk, how it helped me forget things and how it helped me sort through some stuff, at least I thought.

LIVING BUT LOST
CHAPTER 2

I became pregnant at 16 with my first son Jared, and was unsure of who the father could be. When I came home from Job Corps, I was seeing Travis and another guy. I heard Travis had been cheating on me, so I just did the very same thing back; just seemed like the right thing to do, if you got me I was gonna get you. The thing about this was Travis really didn't care about my infidelity. Surprisingly, he wanted to stay with me and help with the baby anyway.

On the one hand, my boyfriend was a drug selling cheater, and on the other hand, I was an unexperienced, premature and mixed up drug user with a premature baby. A baby would not fit into our lifestyle. It would only get in the way. Man, we had no idea what we were doing or about to enter into. I was in no shape for this. I was not ready for this and I sure didn't want to stop partying. I'm thinking my parents partied with us, so I can party with him.

Jared spent more days away from us then he did with us. I would always drop him off with family so they could be responsible and I didn't have to be. Jared spent over half his life with others for nurture and care.

He knows his father but has not had any contact with him from birth. Jared knows some of his dad's family members but has had little communication with them.

My time had run out with the living arrangement of my sister and me. I had to move from her apartment. It was scary. What do you do when you're 17 with no place or family to go to? My grandparents on my father's side were the ones Jared stayed with the most. My grandparents put Jared and me in a one bedroom apartment and paid for us to stay there for a year. Surprisingly enough with Jared being mixed my grandfather took to him immediately. He was crazy about Jared. My grandfather's love for Jared actually opened my own father's eyes to a different view. My grandfather told my dad, his son; "Jared could not help who he was, all you can do is love him." That was huge for my grandfather and even bigger when he shared that with my dad. My grandfather passed away not long after that. Jared was almost one at this time.

The very next year, I became pregnant with my second child, Logan. Here I am an eighteen year old with an addiction, an abusive relationship, lost and hurting on the inside, a toddler and one on the way. Travis and I were two lost souls. We were living together with a kid, a pregnancy, selling and using drugs, and physical abuse. I remember once when Travis, my best friend

Jami, her boyfriend and I were headed for a night out clubbing on another side of town. Travis and I had to stop back by the apartment, and somewhere between the trip to the house and the club, an argument broke out between Travis and me. Travis had punched me in my face so hard that it broke my nose. Blood was everywhere. Jami and her boyfriend went on to the club to wait for us. When we never arrived, Jami decided to go back to the apartment to check on us. As she entered, all she saw was blood, and I was nowhere to be found. She later told me how scared she was because she didn't know if I was dead or alive. All she saw was blood everywhere. We didn't have cell phones back then, so she was left to her thoughts and imagination. That was just one of many situations of abuse I encountered in this relationship; bars after bars after bars. This prison is getting bigger and bigger, appearing to be no way out.

In this period of time my addiction is going from one level to another. Travis and I started to hang around his cousin and her boyfriend a lot. We'll just call her "S" Every day we were at their house. "S" and I would get two gallons of gin a week, limitless supply of cocaine and spend days of no sleep, kids running everywhere and the men hustling. As "S" and I were spending every day together I start noticing her going into her room a lot. Behind the closed doors it was evident that she was doing something more, because a funny smell escaped the crevice each time she was closed in. 'Inquiry mind wants to know,' so I started to ask the right questions and that was the day "S" introduced me to crack cocaine.

Now let me say I've been around it, seen it, touched it and seen others' lives on it and said, 'THAT WILL NEVER BE ME!' I failed miserably. I tried it; crack cocaine and my life was never the same. It was a beast I opened up and could not shut it down. This took me places I never thought I could go; animalistic levels of living, no caution, no care. Travis and I were at the point where either we were going to separate or we were going to kill each other. So I moved out where we were living. In the sickness of drug use, Travis was ok with me and cocaine use but was not going to tolerate me and crack use. After I moved out, my addiction took off to a whole other level. Now, I'm stealing, writing bad checks, using others credit cards, forging their checks and any other criminal activity. I felt like nothing could stop me, and that I was invincible. I would be high, walk into a grocery store and while you were looking on the shelf for your items, I would take your pocket book. Then I had the audacity to use your credit card before leaving and purchase my cigarettes and alcohol with it. I remember leaving my kids in the house during the middle of the night to run to the dope man's house. They were toddlers. I remember putting them in their high chairs in front of the TV so I didn't have to deal with them, or taking them to the baby sitters house. Now to make a bad thing worse, I got pregnant again. What? Yes, that's right a third pregnancy. Darius was inside my belly while all I want to do is get higher and higher. My addiction was in FULL THROTTLE and BY ANY MEANS NECESSARY was the way I lived to get my drugs and trust me; the criminal charges were adding up.

February 18, 1998, I remember lying in a hotel room. The police was looking for me by this time because I had done so much and I called my mother. She could possibly save me or tell me what to do. My mother said to me, "I thought we would hear from you on Tuesday." I was clueless why Tuesday was such a big deal. I didn't understand what this woman was even talking about. Tuesday? And then she says to me, "Heather, Tuesday was Logan's birthday." It was then that I realized I had totally forgotten my daughter's 3rd birthday. I felt like a worthless person. I broke down to tears. My mother said to me, "Heather, you know the police are looking for you. Why don't I come and get you." After contemplating do I go, I agreed. I began to lay there feeling my unborn baby toss and turn in my belly as I waited on my mom. I'm sure he needed water and food. It's the last thing I thought about putting in my body over the past few weeks or even at that moment. She came and took me back where she was living. She fed me, bathed me, let me sleep and then she took me to the police station. I knew when I got there I was going to tell them everything, yes I did it. Here comes a whole new set of prison bars in my life.

STRIVING TO SURVIVE
CHAPTER THREE

I truly believe that those few months I sat in the Lexington County Jail waiting to be accepted into Drug court saved Darius' life. I was able to sleep and eat properly and give my unborn baby nourishment and allow him to grow. When I was released through the drug court program, I didn't want to go backwards again. Travis waited for me to return home so we could pick up being a family again; Darius to be born, with Jared and Logan being a part of the family unit again.

On June 5, 1998, less than a month after I was released from Lexington county jail, our son Darius came into the world. For the first time I felt like I was on my way to recovery. Drug court was a place I went four days a week for intensive treatment along with NA and AA (Narcotics and Alcoholics Anonymous). We met four days a week to start in Phase One, three of those days would be intense group settings and every fourth day, and we went in front of the drug court judge to evaluate our progress for the week. After several months you can move from one phase to the next depending on your contribution in the program.

For the first time in my life, I finally felt like I was

somebody. I started to notice my identity. The 12 steps program helped me understand things about myself and about LIFE as an addict and how to stay clean and sober. This was the answer to my life because it was working; so it seemed. For so long I was what people said I was – *no good*. Travis was my world, so I became whatever Travis said I was.

We had survived for 6 years, because I believed his lies when he said he was the only one that would love me; that no one else would ever want me because I was used up and had three kids. I believed him and settled for the worst. He was only speaking out of his own fiery insecurities. His verbal and physical abuse, promiscuity, and all the other things that came with him was now my ball and chain; my prison sentence. I had to accept there was no way out. He was it, right?

After graduating from drug court and putting my all in N/A (Narcotics Anonymous) I got enough strength to leave. The kids and I left with the clothes on our backs. I was determined to make it. I landed a job at the cell phone shop and it paid great money. I was clean, sober, and living on our own. I was working and going out occasionally to the club scene. I started hanging out with old friends and making new ones. Some of them were doing some of the destructive behaviors I was accustomed to. Our family moved to the projects and I promised myself we wouldn't stay there any longer than we had to, and we didn't. We soon moved out and I got a mobile home, a new car, a motorcycle and things were going well; for a while. I started socializing on the club scene a lot more and bumped up the drinking just a little more. The false confidence settled in and I stopped going to meetings, stopped communicating with my sponsor and convinced myself I was ok. It worked with no drugs for a while but it didn't take long and it picked up where it left off.

IF NOTHING CHANGES, THEN NOTHING CHANGES!

See there's one thing I know, recovery is just that...recovery, but deliverance is deliverance! If nothing changes, then nothing changes.

Travis and I haven't been together in a while but we saw each other from time to time for the kids and our own sinful pleasures. I was hanging with a group of ladies and got introduced to a man who swept me off my feet. We'll just call him Reese. He was very flashy. His lifestyle mimicked the dope game and he loved to spoil me. He would give me money and buy me things all the time. Reese took care of me. His family and I became close and they claimed to love me and I was in deep. My head said I could keep it all, but I was as blind as a bat and foolish enough to think I could live like this. I, with all my power and resources tried really hard not to relapse but who was I kidding; it was all around me again and I was in DEEP with the supplier. I knew where everything was, had access to it all and he didn't care as long as I was happy. This was one of the things therapy warned about in treatment; but it still wasn't enough for me to run the other way.

Pregnant with my 4th child, Kennedy and I was full speed ahead. I used practically my whole pregnancy with Kennedy. Reese would beg me to stop using and when I would be gone for days at a time he would beg for me to come home. I would come back but just to go in his pockets. Reese had wads of money from drug sales and drugs were stashed everywhere and I always knew where to find it. Reese had his own demons of using cocaine also. It was easy to manipulate Reese when he was high. One thing I can say he never drew his hand to strike me about anything.

I went into early labor because of my using. I remember the day as I was high I kept leaking fluid all over the place as if I were urinating and I knew that couldn't be right. Previously, I stole dope and money from Reese and ran out, but didn't want to go back home. I had to get to the emergency room. I knew I needed to be checked and when I got there they immediately saw the problem. I was high and I had been for a few days at this point and was leaking amniotic fluid. They called the Doctor in and they said that I needed to deliver. They alerted me the Department of Social Services (DSS) would be involved. Kennedy was born and placed under observation. When Kennedy would come off the drugs he would not be going home with me alone. DSS placed us on a placement agreement with Reese's mother and I was allowed to stay in the house with them, but it was still no good for me. The dragon was out and I couldn't contain him. I was still using and leaving every chance I got to get high. Yet again another set of bars, DSS.

My mother was living in Charleston SC just hours away and asked me to come and stay with her and my step-father. Jared and Darius were already living with them while Logan was with Travis' cousin. I knew I couldn't break free with Reese so I said yes and DSS agreed to set up the placement with my mom. I would drive back and forth to see Reese and bring Kennedy with me. It was against protocol but my mother allowed it anyway. Acting out of love, she just wanted to keep me from doing wrong. Having Kennedy with me and letting us see Reese would help only one trip there, I never made it back. I went to get high and didn't stop until I was caught by the police. The story as it unfolds looks like this.

I had my mother's only car and I was two hours away from Charleston. I left mother at work, with no way to get home and I left Jared and Darius in day care with no way for anyone to get them. Kennedy was left at his dad's; where he and I were not supposed to be. I was MIA (missing in action) getting high. My mother had no choice but to call DSS and let them know. They picked Kennedy up from his dad's and placed him into foster care and charged me with child endangerment. I was in trouble all over again.

I was a fugitive, scared with my mother's only car and all I wanted to do was mask the pain. This was the stage that for the first time, I see this sickness in my disease. The silence is screaming to my conscience, 'How could you do this Heather? What is wrong with you?' I didn't have any answers, but what I had was broken any so called relationships with my family members; my sister, my brother. My dad was tired of bailing me out of the county jails.

It was like 'Ok Heather, when enough is going to be enough?' After being on the run again from probation, pardon and parole I was finally caught. I was escorted back to the county jail in Charleston and sat there until my court date. After sitting there for a couple months, the court reinstated my probation and my new charges ran into my already pending probation sentence.

I kept wondering how in the world I keep getting through the system with a couple months of county time and back to probation? The court offered me to go in a program for mothers. There would be DSS involvement, but it would allow the kids to stay with me and for us to get help as a family. This treatment was five days a week; the kids went to therapeutic child care (TCU) while I was in class. With completion of the program we could transition into our own place and my record would be expunged; so I accepted.

Darius was not yet in kindergarten when I started and he got to stay at TCU all day. When I would drop him off he would scream and scream. The teachers told me how he would scream while I was gone, and knew there was a deeper issue. There were times they had to get me out of class just so he could see my face. We believed Darius was suffering from separation anxiety. That he was so scared I was going to leave him again and not come back. Every morning I would have to give him the key to our room to bring him some comfort and give him a sense of peace that I was going to return.

The Mothers Program was a wonderful program and it helped me in more ways than one for quite some time. The values of being a drug free parent and also a productive member of society were great accomplishments. I did graduate from the program and we transitioned to our own place. Surely my children and I were well on our way. I will say this time there was a difference than any other times I had gone through treatment; t was the first time ever I was introduced to Jesus Christ.

I made a confession of faith while in step ahead. There was a couple named Willy & Chris Pace who came into the program once a week for Bible study for anyone who wanted to attend. We would go to their church on Sundays and I began to ask questions. I didn't get the whole Christian thing, but something sounded good, and I needed help. I didn't know anything about God's word. I thought Noah's Ark was what people decorated their kids nursery's with, I had no idea it was biblical. I didn't grow up with a family who was saved, went to church or even practiced being the church. Remember I was born into a family that was in bondage and in captivity. So I had so many questions. Chris and I would spend time together even outside of Bible studies on campus. My hunger for change had me insatiably inquisitive. I was able to ask questions and she gave me the best answers according to my level of understanding. Our group was able to lean on her if there were questions and she and her husband would pour into us. I'm so very thankful for their obedience to the call. Although Willy has passed away, I will never forget Chris and Willy. Until this day I give God thanks for them.

As the kids and I were slowly building our lives

together, we transitioned out of the program into our own place. I am working every day, the kids are in daycare and school, I have help managing my money and I'm still attending meetings; but here we go again. I started hanging out with the wrong crowd all over again. I met a guy and started letting him stay overnight with us, I started to let him sell drugs from our apartment and I started to occasionally use from time to time. Because I wasn't all the way in the clear with DSS I would have unscheduled visits from my guardian et litem and case worker from time to time and I remember one day they showed up and I didn't know what to do.

I had put some clean urine in an eye dropper bottle in case they would ever pop a drug test on me. I told the kids to take Kennedy up stairs and stay in their room. My kids already knew something was up when I decided to let this guy come as he pleased, smoke cigarettes and sleep in my bed.

When the case worker told me she needed a urine sample I was so nervous and fidgety. I tried to use my own rigged up sample but it didn't work. The test came back positive and they took the kids back out of the house. The devastating looks on their faces is something not soon forgotten. The older ones faces of anger and hurt, saying, 'How could you do this again to us?' The younger ones cry; not knowing or understanding what was happening. They cried and cried for me to go with them but I just couldn't. Here I am again at a place of despair and hopelessness and it was truly no one's fault but my own. As months went by, and I was getting high, letting this guy live with me, forfeiting all my housing rights; I get a call from my mom that she and my sister were coming to visit. That was unusual because my sister had nothing to do with me for some time. When they arrived they shared the news that Travis had been killed. That moment a piece of me was ripped away from my heart and right there, I wanted to die along with him. I truly couldn't handle my pain. Grief was way too much for me. I felt mad, guilty, sad, and every other emotion that is categorized with grief. Not knowing there was a comfort of the Holy Spirit, I was lost and hopeless with misery. I just wanted a chance to see Travis and ask him to forgive me and beg for the opportunity so we could get it right. I was trapped in a place feeling guilty that I left him, my kids are gone, I'm getting ready to be homeless and I'm all out of options. Maybe if I hadn't gone, he might still be alive. What am I to do, I just want life to be over with.

As we had to go back to Columbia for the funeral, I was trying to mask the pain with all the drugs I could and I was on a suicide mission trying to do it. My mother, the kids and I headed to the funeral. It was way too much for me to bear. I had to stay behind in Columbia to sort through everything and my mother had to get the kids back to start school that following week.

Recalling that day I went back to the house Travis and I bought and lived in together. As I walked in it was just like I left it when we lived there. The table was still set with the same dishes; the towels I decorated the bathroom with were still in place just the way I left it. The pictures I put on the wall were still in the same places, and some of my clothes were still left in the closet. At this point I lost it completely. It was fresh all over again and it hit me like a boulder. It felt like I was still living there because no other woman had ever taken my place. If she had, she would have made it her own. I was truly shattered and distraught in more ways than one.

Needless to say, again I never made it back to Charleston until the police brought me back. It seems to be the story of my life. My mother had my children again. Kennedy was back in foster care and I was on a dark mission of suicide. I wanted the drugs to kill me or this lifestyle to take me out. I have lost my first love, my kids have lost their father, and I certainly have abandoned them and I just wanted to die; and I truly didn't care how. I had had enough of life's heart aches;

surrendering to take no more. More bars I'm creating for myself and now for my own children. I drank and I smoked 'til I could take no more and then I would do it all over again. This went on for six months. I was living in abandoned buildings, eating out of the trash, walking in a fog on the streets day in and day out. I was trafficked out by men and I was being abused, raped and beaten every day; animalistic living, any and everything goes at this point.

I was forced in the car with a man by my pimp who kidnapped me. Now, I was hoping for a way to make some money or at least get high by being forced in this car, but he had a whole other agenda in mind. This guy had recently been in a car accident with an 18 wheeler and had open cuts all over his face and body. I remember thinking to myself, this is unsafe and unsanitary, but who cares. After we got my drug of choice, he brought me to a hotel room. I asked him for a shower. After saying yes, he asked me for the pipe I smoked on. I was just going to wait until I got out of the shower to get high myself, I gathered he smoked weed but didn't know of anything else. When we got the drugs, I figured they were for me; not him. When I got out of the shower, I found him getting high on my pipe. I didn't really know what to expect but I went with the flow. After about thirty minutes in, he transformed and locked me in the room and had me to lie naked on the bed with every piece of furniture against the door. He began to beat me and raped me repeatedly. He was getting high in the process of taking all he wanted from me and held me captive like this for four days. During this time I begged him to let me go. The higher he got the scarier it got for me. I just didn't know what he was capable of. I laid there in the middle of the bed exposed and vulnerable, my hands out to my side, legs straight down and he dared me to move. If I twitched he thought I was taking something from him and he would beat me. If I moved a millimeter at any position; my head, fingers or toes he would begin to beat me because he was insanely paranoid. While getting high, he would at a moment's notice want sexual activity and forced me to do things to him. He was clammy from his stench sweat, and sooty from the smoke and ashes. He had been digging in the carpet, the trash and the ceiling tiles; so he was extremely nasty.

Now I may be in a hopeless state in my life, and wanted to die, but not today! I must have found a piece of survival way down on the inside. He soon ran out of

Now I may be in a hopeless state in my life, and wanted to die, but not today! I must have found a piece of survival way down on the inside.

dope and no one would come to bring him more. I had no way of a phone or a way to leave, and FEAR had become my best friend! At this point I was scared for my life even though I was helpless in what I could do. When he decided to leave the room to get more dope, the *fighter* in me woke up and the *flight rescuer* took over because I knew this was my chance to GET OUT.

I convinced him to get something else to get high with; He knew I had connections with drug dealers because of the influence when he purchased me from my pimp. As we approached the area and I knew who to talk to. The guy I got drugs from asked me where had I been and why haven't they seen me? This was the area Kennedy's dad was from so they knew I had been missing, and the pimp who sold me out that night told others I never came back. I told the dope boy what happened to me. He went up to the car of the man and threatened him with his gun and took his money. The guy got scared and took off. When some of the people found out what had happened to me, they wanted me to file a police report. Contrary to their defense, I was as much at fault as he in the first place. My pimp threatened my life to carry out this awful act, so I just had to let it go. It amazes me how guilt, fear and shame will keep us locked in our sin.

After being on the run again for several months, I was

caught by the police and returned back to the probation department after sitting in the county jail again. I was really struggling with death demons and just really wanted to die or did I? What is this war inside me? However I was back at hopelessness again and I didn't want to live anymore. Why won't I die?

While in the county jail this time, things from the past of being at church and in Bible study started coming back to me. Now I had a cell-mate tell me to read *Proverbs 3:5-6*. *"Trust in The Lord with all your heart and lean not on your own understanding, but in all your ways acknowledge Him and He shall direct your path."* I recall that sticking with me but not fully understanding what it meant.

You can probably imagine by now, I have burnt every single bridge I had and no one is listening to me anymore. I truly felt alone as if no one was on my side and everyone had given up on me. But one thing I did was request a Bible from the bookshelf from the officers. I became faithful about reading it every day; even though I didn't understand anything I was reading.

After sitting in jail for a few months, I was called back to court. Once again, I was released to probation and placed into the Restitution Center. The Restitution Center is a place where one works and the income earned go towards fees, fines and restitution. After being there for some time, one can get passes to go home on the weekends. Let me remind you that my mother has two of my boys and has lost her marriage; moved back to Columbia. My daughter is with her dad's family and Kennedy is in foster care.

Meanwhile, I had missed every foster care review board hearing for my son Kennedy and because of that I lost all my parental rights to him. He was placed into the DSS foster care system and even if I could prove that I had changed and gotten myself together, those rights were terminated when I chose not to show up. In the restitution center you work and pay your money to them and you get passes to go home on the weekends. Well on my job that's where I met a guy we will call him "T" He became a big part of my passes on the weekend. I would spend time with his family he with mine. I became consumed by him. I was able to see him every day when I went to work and the weekends for my passes.

He spoke a lot about *GOD*. His mother and step father were in ministry. I thought to myself, he seems different from all the rest. Surely he is the one and will be good to me. We were sexually active while at work and weekends and as a result of our sexual activity, I got pregnant. When I found out I had to leave the center, I moved back to my mother's house where Jared and Darius were. I was dismissed because the policy of the Restitution Center did not uphold pregnancy. Nonetheless, I believed that I had found the real antidote and life would now be good. I was clean, he loved *GOD* and this was going to be it.

Living with my mother was never easy or good for either of us. We tried, but we did not get along at all, so she kicked me out; and truth is I wanted to leave "T" and I decided we were going to live together. We had NOTHING of ourselves, but some of his friends allowed us to move in with them. We stayed there for just a short period of time and then moved into our own place. It was a little one bedroom apartment in downtown Columbia by the University. Truth is I had a sugar daddy that helped me out a lot and he put me in this place in his name and paid the rent for a year, all I had to do was be available when he called and wanted to see me for sexual favors. I was in some kind of wonderland for sure.

"T" was working for a temp agency periodically and I was working within walking distance at Subway. We had one car which my mother gave to me. We were trying to make a go at it; at least half of us; me. One day I started questioning some of his very strange behaviors like: Why wasn't he sleeping? Why was he coming in late? Why wasn't he eating? Why was his phone always going off? Why was he so secretive? I experienced this behavior in past relationships. I first assumed he may have been cheating on me. One day I came home from work due to sickness from the pregnancy. He used the car for work and I used to walk since I was moments away from my job. As I approached the house, I saw the car leave the driveway. I thought he might've come home for lunch or something, but when I walked in the house, I notice the patio door open. I went to investigate and discovered drugs and paraphernalia on the patio table. I was tricked and devastated again! My heart was broken again and I knew how this story was going to end. I picked up the house phone to call his cell phone and noticed his voice. Now it all made sense to me. I didn't let him know that he had been found out, but when he finally got home; his bag was packed with the little he had and ALL he had left on the patio while getting high.

He became belligerent. He beat and choked me until I couldn't breathe. "T" told me he wasn't going anywhere and neither was I. Even though I was pregnant, it did not stop him from fighting me. His manipulation got worse over the months. He would kick and throw me like I was a rag doll. He made me pay all the bills anyway that meant, walking the streets to working for a service or call my sugar daddy to. I'm back getting high, pregnant, and in abusive relationship while working selling my body. There would be times I was scared to come home; not knowing what state he was in or if my unborn baby and I would end up dead.

One night "T" threatened to kill me if I didn't get him the money he owed the dope man. I didn't have any money so he threw me across the room. When he did, my water broke. I asked him several times to take me to the emergency room, but he wouldn't. He had the keys to the car and wouldn't let me leave. Even through his rage and anger, I made it to the ER. I was only seven and a half months at the time and they did all they could to keep my baby from coming. I was placed on bed rest in the hospital until they couldn't stop her from coming any longer. Ava-Grace was born by Cesarean Section weighing four pounds and positive for drugs. Here we go again; the cycle of my life: more DSS, more bars, will this ever end?

SWIMMING UPSTREAM
CHAPTER FOUR

Have you ever watched a river flow? For the most part it is consistent in movement. The flow can be mesmerizing watching from the sidelines. It's so inviting that you must take a swim. You're going along enjoying the swim, and without notice, an alteration in movement changes the whole dynamic of your swim. Now a fight is on because you're being pulled in by a current. It is always easier to go with the flow of current, but you must consciously make a decision to move against the current. Swimming upstream is nearly impossible, but with the right tools, it is doable. My life over the years was a constant battle: it was like swimming upstream.

Getting out of the relationship with "T" was life threatening. I came home from the hospital and never went back to see Ava. Ava was there in the Neonatal Intensive Care (NIC) Unit for 3 months and her paternal grandmother was there every morning, noon, day and night to love on her and pray over her. "T" and I were in a love war that seemingly would end in someone's death. I finally left the night when he put seven staples in the side of my head. I went to a new city to hide from the Jekyll and Hyde monster in "T" I knew if he found me he would once again try to take life from me in every way possible.

One day a girl I ran the streets with was leaving her apartment, and "T" was staking me out from the back of another house, as we left he started to follow us. I thought I was a little safer considering I was in public and lots of people were out and about. We kept walking and he kept yelling, trying to get me to come to him. I kept telling my friend, we can't stop. She knew how abusive he was from my past experiences with black eyes, busted lips and strangle marks around my neck; she was scared as well. As we were walking he was asking me for a cigarette, I continued to ignore him plus the fact I did not have one to give him. We came up to the Greyhound bus station where I saw a city police parked out front. I thought he may pull off because he didn't want to cause suspicion with the police; but that wasn't the case. After getting a cigarette from someone at the bus station, He walked up and snuck me from behind and punched me in my face so hard that I fell to the ground. I don't remember much after that, but being on the stretcher on the way to the ER feeling like I was being smothered. When I came to, I was at the hospital and had a concussion. As I came to I could see my mother was there with me. She said I had an MRI and my nose was broken the second time and there were seven staples in the side of my head. "T" was arrested as the police witnessed it all. He didn't seem to care about the authorities looking. It was almost as if he wanted them to know I deserved it. When this hulk came alive, I knew he meant to kill me. It happened on more occasions than I could count. He simply just did not care. You're talking to one hurt, angry, lost little girl who has so much shame and guilt that life didn't seem real any longer. I couldn't see any hope nor did I believe I deserved any.

The cycle continued as I ran from life, my responsibilities, myself, and it was not over yet. With a life full of hurt by others and hurt I caused myself, I desired to be in a better place and have a more disciplined lifestyle but had no clue how to obtain it. The only hope I got was when I would be incarcerated. I would attend Bible study groups that came in from the outside, but when I would leave it was right back to where I left off. I didn't get it. Why was this? There had to be a reason I was still here. I should have been dead so many times. Why am I still alive?

Between all the bad choices and behaviors; my children were crying for me, asking me to stay with them. Darius had severe separation disorder attaching him to me. Knowing I was going to leave him again, I came around less as possible. Jared was acting out, being tossed back and forth from my mother to grandmother... He had some identity issues not understanding his skin color; Jared didn't know if he was black or white. My grandmother who he lived with was prejudice and telling him things that confused him, along with the fact that his real dad wanted nothing to do with him, and I was also an absentee parent. He resulted in attempts of death wishes; fantasizing with suicide. Logan was not happy. She was grieving her father's death and didn't understand why I wouldn't come get her. Kennedy is stuck in foster care. Mother would go see him regularly and tried to adopt him. He had behavioral issues that the foster care family would not tolerate. Kennedy is super hyperactive and has a lot of energy. After doing the proper protocol for adoption, Kennedy was finally adopted by my mother. Glory be to God! He is with family. The bars I continued to place myself in are getting deeper and deeper, but I've started a way for my children to have life behind bars also.

LOOKING FOR DRY LAND
CHAPTER FIVE

Well my rope had finally gotten shorter; from violating my probation, losing my daughter Ava, to drug use and prostitution, and so many other things. I was faced with going back to jail, but this time to the 'Big House' - the South Carolina Department of Corrections. The judge sentenced me one year and gave me county time in order to be there for about five and a half months. There was a secret place inside me leaping for joy to go back to confinement because now I could stay clean and attempt to get myself together; or somewhat. I remember being in the Reception & Evaluation place. R & E is a holding center before you are assigned to the compound you would be brought to.

I was in a room with two other females during this process. This is a cell that has two bunks in it, a mat on the floor, two small strips of window with no view, a steel metal toilet with a sink attached, and a slot in the door big enough for receiving food, medicine or mail. The doors are locked from the outside and you are gathered with other offenders. At this point, all offenders are classified the same, murderers were housed with bad check writers. No matter what the offense and sentence, everyone is grouped together and there is nothing you can do about it.

Outside ministries are allowed to come in and share the Gospel during the week. They would stand in the middle of the building, yelling out as we put our ears at the feeding slot, and sometimes they were allowed to pray with us. On this particular day the ministry came in to pray with us. I could hear them praying for the person before me, knowing I would be next. But in an instant the time for ministry was up, therefore I didn't get my personal prayer with the ministers. I was disappointed to say the least, because I really wanted them to pray for me. As the lady passed my door, she paused to look at me square in the eyes and said while pointing to me, "You, come here." She continued, "You have to press through. You have to press through! Just like the woman with the issue of blood, you'd better press through!"

While she was saying these things, she was pounding her fist against the inside of her hand. Every time she emphasized **press through**. She did it with her fist against the other hand. I had no idea what she was talking about. I asked my roommate (Bay) an older Christian woman, "Do you know what she was talking about? What is the lady with the issue of blood all about?" She tells me the story, and then she read it to me from *Luke 8:43-48*.

⁴³And a woman was there who had been subject to bleeding for twelve years, [a]but no one could heal her. ⁴⁴She came up behind him and touched the edge of his cloak, and immediately her bleeding stopped. ⁴⁵"Who touched me?" Jesus asked. When they all denied it, Peter said, "Master, the people are crowding and pressing against you." ⁴⁶But Jesus said, "Someone touched me; I know that power has gone out from me." ⁴⁷Then the woman, seeing that she could not go unnoticed, came trembling and fell at his feet. In the presence of all the people, she told why she had touched him and how she had been instantly healed. ⁴⁸Then he said to her, "Daughter, your faith has healed you. Go in peace."

I thought about what the minister reinforced in me for quite some time. I asked the Lord to bring it back to my memory later.

I still didn't fully understand what this meant for me and why I was picked out of the three of us in the room. This was beyond me, but it sure did give me cause to ponder over the next couple years.

When I left R & E, I made every chapel service and Bible study available and so much started fitting together for me. The things I heard from Willy & Chris Pace that once came into the program to share the Gospel, things at church, in the county jail services and my cell-mate when she gave me *Proverb3:5-6*. I felt like everywhere I turned there were scriptures I had heard or read and then every time I turned on the Christian radio station, the Lord was speaking to me through songs. I know now that it's the Lord's way of pursuing us.

One of the ladies who came into the prison talked about speaking those things that are not as if they were. She said to visualize what it is I wanted in life. Well I began to visualize, then I drew pictures of me and my kids with a big house as a family. The kids were always on the right side of the picture playing. Logan and Ava-Grace were always on a swing set, the boys were always playing baseball. There was an animal in the picture with them and I was always on a bench reading. I visualized a two story house with a long driveway. On the other side of the house were flowers with my mom, a big tree and a bright shining sun. I wrote on the top of every picture like that

Matthew 6:33 Seek ye first the Kingdom of God and His righteousness and all shall be added unto you."

I had no idea what I was doing, but I did what I heard, later learning that's how faith works and that was God's spirit speaking to me. There was so much information downloaded in my head during this time, I just needed to know it was all real and it was all true. Although I was behind prison bars, there was something taking

root in me that was so freeing.

As I received my job assignment for work release, I got assigned to yard maintenance. One day while we were at work, a group of us ladies were all raking leaves together. Some were talking about being an addict and made the comment, "Once you're an addict, you're always an addict." that spoke loudly as WRONG to me; it just did not sound right to me anymore. I've always heard that in all the different treatment places, but this time it just sounded wrong.

So I went to a place where I was raking leaves by myself, and I heard someone speak to me but no one was around. I looked all around me to see who was there and saw no one. I knew I had heard someone say, "You are a new creature!" I didn't know who or what that was, I've heard people say that the Holy Spirit talks to them so I wondered, was that Holy Spirit? And why would He talk to me? I went back to raking till it was time to go. When I got back to my dorm, I grabbed a Kenneth Copeland book off the shelf put it on my bunk and took my shower. I got ready for dinner and Bible study, and then came for count and lights out. While on my bunk, picked the book up, turned on my lap and the very first chapter I opened to read was *2 Corinthians 5:17 "Therefore if anyone is in Christ, he is a new creation; old things have passed away, behold all things have become new."*

I knew at that very moment I heard the Holy Spirit. The Holy Spirit really had spoken to me when I was cleaning and raking the grounds. The amazing thing was the voice was not unfamiliar. I heard that same voice and sound when I was little and everyone told me I was crazy.

IN OVER MY HEAD
CHAPTER SIX

fter doing my county and state time behind bars for over a year, it was time for my release. I have a planned to move back in with my mom and boys. I had lost my parental rights to Kennedy who was adopted by mom and I could have access to Logan and Ava-Grace. It was going to be good this time, my intentions were good and I was putting my best foot forward. All I wanted was to be healthy and whole; only the problem was that I had not fully surrendered my life yet. I thought I had, but the truth was told when I decided to hold on to old people, places and things. I didn't like living with my mom because it brought back so many hurts I couldn't let go from childhood. There was still resentment harboring in me for her. I saw her as my enemy and she saw me as hers.

I just knew I would get a job and I would take my children, move out, and live happily ever after, but it wasn't long before my former influences of my past started to make life look easier and it placed the pipe right back in my mouth and on a downward spiral I go. There is a saying that your addiction always picks up where it left off. It was true for me. Back to the races we go, and it NEVER gets better.

I was on the run again from Probation Pardon and Parole Services, my addiction was off the charts, my kids became last again and I worked for an escort service placing myself in so much jeopardy. My kids and other family members were mad and disappointed in me; I was covered with guilt and shame but didn't have the ability I needed to stop. I was on the run again because I knew my probation was violated and the police would be looking for me.

In December of 2007, a female that worked and ran the streets with me, collided into a tree head on with a client's car. It all happened so fast that I didn't even know what happened. All I remember was the girl I was working with left me for dead; ran off with my purse, cash and drugs. I was unconscious and in a lot of pain and all I remember waking up in the hospital with a morphine drip. I couldn't move; my hip and pelvis was fractured and I was in and out of consciousness from the morphine. There were police at my door and reminded me there was no way I was leaving without them. I was going to the county with new charges and with the violation of my probation.

Can my life get any worse and at this point did I really even care? I was not ready to surrender to my addiction, Jesus, or the authorities but whatever needed to happen, so be it. Christmas day 2008, I was discharged with no police escort. They made a mistake so I made a mad dash, but I was in no way finished; my addiction was suffering and so was I. I truly had no place to go, my dad and I hadn't lived together since I was fifteen, no other family would support me and knowing my mom's house would be the first place the police would look for me, I went right back to ol' familiar; the dope house.

What a vicious cycle of animalistic living I was in, I couldn't even walk and here I was still walking in my self-will. I had a porta potty beside my bed with bed chucks under me because I could barely move to make it to the bathroom. There would be days before someone would stop by to help me. Believe me, when you're not the life of the party or when you get in a vulnerable state, you find out you have no friends and everyone gets gone. I couldn't get to physical therapy because the police may find me there, so I suffered pain and stayed hidden.

I was so sick in my addiction that was suffering that I came to the place where I called those who needed sexual favors to come by so I could make a few dollars to get a fix. This was desperation at its lowest; by any means necessary. As time went on, I forced myself to get up and walk with my walker. I believe because of my determination not to let this stop or slow me down,

I might not be walking today.

I was not going to stop using because I just wasn't ready to quit. What was it going to take; jails, institutions and death? Was it going to have to be death? It's the only thing that hasn't happened and heck I've tried that so many different times and so many different ways. I knew the police were looking for me and I got scared they would find me, so I went back to Charleston. Having already been familiar with the area and had been gone long enough to be missed by the streets, I was just like new money to them, fresh meat; and so it was. I didn't have too much to live for; hope wasn't looking very good for me and I JUST DIDN'T CARE.

The streets and I took full advantage of each other. Because I was the new kid; the fresh meat on the block, that gave me an upper hand on using and being used. So I used it till I was all used up. Once again, ANYTHING and EVERTHING goes. I was living between motels being pimped out as he supplied the drugs and I lived day to day to support my habit.

I got involved with a new escort service and met different people. This one guy introduced me to his brother who lived in the Hamptons in New York. We talked by telephone and it was a hit. The brother said he had produced a new cigarette and wanted me to fly there and drive back down to Charleston making stops in-between to sale his product. He wanted to buy my plane ticket plus hire me for $8000. I would get half up front and the other half when done. "Agreed," I said. The guy who I worked for said yes also. He warned me to be quiet and not to ask any questions. The less I knew the better off I would be. He believed this guy could be in the Mafia and I needed to be eye candy for him to do whatever he was doing.

I saw it as a business deal and I was all in. The guy did what he said, bought my ticket and sent me $4000 by western union. I was getting out of South Carolina and I was ok with that. I needed a fresh start; I was in Charleston long enough, the police were looking for me, and I had been used up by everyone around me. This was just another set of bars placed around the prison of my life.

The morning I was to fly out of Charleston to New York, I was a little scared because I knew I was wanted by the police and my name was on the ticket. Did anyone even care? Did I even really care? The night prior to leaving, I went to Walmart to get a luggage bag and ran into one of the girls I frequently got high with. She asked me for a ride and I knew I wanted to get one last fix before I left. As we entered her neighborhood, I saw the police get behind me, and I just KNEW THIS WAS IT. I honestly had already made up my mind when I got caught this time; it was going to be OVER once and for all. I looked at the girl and said to her, "If you have anything on you, give it to me because I know I am going to jail." She handed me her pipe and all the stuff she had on her. As the police approached the car, I remember for the first time EVER feeling at PEACE. Yes I was going to jail, but I did NOT care. I knew on the inside of me that that part of my life was finally over.

I can't really explain it all, as the police approached my window and although I had 10 names I could have given to them to get out of what I was in, I said to him, my name is Heather Ann Pounds. This is my social security number, my date of birth and I told him I was wanted by the South Carolina Pardon and Parole Services. I handed him everything I had and told him thank you. To the officer's surprise; and he was definitely caught off guard by my willingness to surrender. As they asked us both to get out of the vehicle, I asked the officer could he please let my friend go. "I was just giving her a ride home and she had nothing to do with what was going on with me." After checking her out, he let her walk away and didn't charge her with anything. As the woman police officer came to search me and put me in her car, I knew they were just trying to figure out why I had done what I did. Why would I be so willing to surrender?

The female Police officer placed me in the backseat of her car and as we were driving to the police station, I cried out over and over, "Thank You Lord, Thank You Lord, Thank You Lord!" She kept looking at me in the mirror and asked me if I was ok? I told her, "I had never been better." When we got to the police station, the male officer that stopped me initially had to book me. He was puzzled asking, "Why didn't you try to run or get out of this?" I simply said to him, "Because I AM TIRED AND IT IS OVER."

BEAUTY FOR ASHES
CHAPTER SEVEN

There was something in me that BROKE the night of August 24th 2008. Everything started to come together. Even in the midst of the fog, I could see so clearly. I truly believe if I'd gotten on that plane, I would not be here today; I would've been killed. That might have been a human trafficking situation I never would've survived. Being in Charleston County jail with new charges, having to wait to be extradited back to Columbia for violation of probation, there was a calm I could not explain. I was at a place of perfect peace. I didn't care how much time I was going to do, I was ok with whatever was in front of me because it was better than what was behind me.

For the first time ever I understood what it meant to FULLY SURRENDER physically, emotionally and spiritually. It was time to take everything in my head and have God write it on the tables of my heart. The emotional and mental bars I lived behind all my life, is the physical and spiritual bars I'd live behind for the next couple years. Little did I know these bars would actually SET ME FREE from all the entrapments I placed over my own heart and life.

The first few weeks were hardest because I was so drained; completely depleted! I couldn't even stay awake to go to bond court, to eat or to shower. I was worn out physically, mentally and spiritually that all I could do was sleep. This was detoxing for me. I remember when I went to bond court the judge sent me back to my room because I couldn't keep my eyes open or stand up. I had run myself ragged in the streets. For months, I existed in comatose condition. Eventually I went to bond court and was given a bond that I couldn't make or that I even wanted to make if I could.

It was time for me to sit still. I had to stay for 90 days for DUS #4 (driving under suspension) and paraphernalia charges, and I waited for Lexington County Pardon and Parole to book me for new violations and charges and I was ok with every bit of it. I had never felt better in my life. I may have been in Prison behind bars, but I was FREE INSIDE for the first time in my life. I just KNEW THIS was the beginning of a NEW ME!! What I heard that day raking those leaves was true, I am a new creature and Christ has everything to do with it.

When I repented asking God to forgive me and help me not go back, He dealt with me, and I began to listen. I began to see and hear so much clearer. I was at a place of peace and I was in a place of confinement with no distractions. The Holy Spirit was speaking to me and I could hear Him clearly.

God started speaking to me by showing me numbers and kept showing me the number 5. Where I begin to look around, I noticed the number 5 everywhere. The number 5 was the inmate ID number and on the cell I was assigned to. I met a woman years back named Irene. We both shared a lot in common. She also had past addiction issues and we would always see one another when we were in the county jail. One day we were walking in Rec and she told me that 5 was the number of grace. That brought me deeper after I kept seeing it over and over. As I began to think of my life and the number 5, I saw it repeatedly. I was born in May, the 5th month; I have 5 children and my 5th child's name is Ava-Grace. This again brought more comfort, more peace and increased my faith knowing the Lord was with me and was speaking to me. This is how He began to grow my faith, as I started to see Him in everything around me.

After several months, it came time to leave Charleston and go to Lexington to face what was ahead. I was certain God was with me; certainly He wasn't going to leave me now. I was booked in Lexington County Jail and placed in the housing area, surprisingly enough I was assigned to pod #5. Man, this just increased my faith and peace even greater! I had no idea how long I would be incarcerated, I just knew it didn't matter. I was ready and willing to do whatever needed to be done to get this behind me, to move ahead and beyond the bars.

I was listening to Holy Spirit as I was standing at the bookshelf one day and there were slips of paper laying there. The Holy Spirit impressed upon me to write Bible verses on them and hand them out to others; so I did. This allowed me to bless others, while being engaged in His Word. As I was giving the strips of Bible verses to others in my unit, they would come up to me and talk; asking if we could have Bible study together in the multipurpose room. After getting permission, we met any chance we could.

We were allowed to come out twice a day for an hour each time to shower and have recreation; that is if everyone listened so that privileges weren't taken away. Our time became very powerful and encouraging to one another. This is where the Holy Spirit started to show me BROKENNESS, EMPTINESS & LONELINESS in women like myself. We had all these things in common; #1We were all still alive, and were saved and spared for a reason; #2 we all needed a smidgen of hope to get through; #3 we all had been in search of love our whole lives and need the Savior.

I committed to a group study called Celebrate Recovery. It's a Christ centered 12 step program that required eight weeks attendance. I knew I would be there the required time or longer, so I committed. I was able to glean a lot from the sessions; and it helped to deal with hurts, habits and hang-ups used by the 12 steps of NA and AA but with biblical principles. I was familiar with this from when I was in treatment in Charleston years before.

At this point a lot has happened to me mentally, physically and spiritually. I was delivered and God was teaching me how to now stay free, because it says in John 8:36 "So if the Son sets you free, you will be free indeed." No program could do it any longer, I didn't need a temporary fix, and I needed a permanent solution to my life's issues. I needed Jesus to deliver and set me free ONCE and FOR ALL.

As I sat waiting on my court date I just wanted to draw closer and closer to God. I finally understood what others had told me about abiding in God's word, standing on His word, and living in His word. It all made sense to me for the very first time.

Finally I got a court date and name of the judge that would hear my case. It was the same judge who sentenced me the first time and told me he'd better never see me again. This prompted me to pray for him. I never asked the Lord to keep me from prison, I just asked for His will to be done for me. I knew many times before, I prayed He would get me out of the mess I made but when He did, I messed it all up again. I didn't want to do the same thing I had always done. I was looking at ten years for my violation and for my new charges, and I truly was ok with that.

It was Wednesday in December. My name was called for court. The original date given me would fall on Friday but I could not worry; I had to trust The Lord. I went in front of the judge and he asked me if I had any requests. I told him that I was not able to communicate with my mother about the court date change and I really wanted her there. The judge showed me favor by saying, "If I can see you today, I can see you Friday." I was pleasingly surprised. You see my mother always came to all my court hearings; no matter how many times I was jailed. Not that it would make a difference in the decision making process, it was just having her there made the difference for me and made me feel better. As I got back to the jail and in my dorm, I began to thank God for His favor. The Holy Spirit led me to write a letter to the judicial system. In this letter I poured my heart out, taking responsibility for all the years I had messed up. Thanking them for all their help and apologizing to them for always taking the Probation, Pardon and Parole services for granted. I was unsure why I wrote this letter. Did I just need to write it for myself or to share with them during court?

As I slept on it, prayed over it and shared it with the Bible study group. I was sure that I should share it at court.

Friday had come; the wait was over and it was time to face the music. Whatever the outcome, it was definitely the start to a new beginning in my life. I remember getting the call from the dorm at around 3:00 a.m.; I was then taken to the booking area where I am always very cold. The booking area was actually a cell with a steal toilet and sink with lots of other people who were there for court also.

This was one of the hardest places to be because of the darkness and depression all around you. You got a brown bag with a cold PBJ sandwich and warm carton of milk. It was a cheap and calculated meal. Although I was in a good place in my soul, this was certainly no fancy-ritzy treatment of a five star hotel; it was still JAIL. Our name is called, and we are lined up facing the wall. This is where shackles are put on our feet, and chains bind us all together, from one end to the next. If humiliation has not stolen the last bit of gall and unction from you, turning you around making sure your hands are cuffed and locked will just about do it. After making sure we are really who we say we are by the number given on our wrist bands, we are then shuffled to a van that's separated by metal; keeping males on one side and females on the other. The van had an unpleasant odor to say the least; it smelled like urine, body odor and filth, reminding me of the solitary confinement when I was in as a teenager. If you could hold your breath for the ride, you were doing well; not to mention all the remarks coming from the men on the other side acting like wild animals.

With the fate to be determined in the hallowed halls, the pitiful bagged lunch, a bus filled with raunchy smells, and vulgarity, we are finally at the court house. Again we were placed in a holding cell, much like the one I described before, waiting and waiting for court to take place. I would comfort myself by singing the little songs I learned from chapel services, or continually recalled scriptures to my mind. Court is finally now in session and it's been a LONG morning. When brought to the court room, you are sat on the front row. You cannot look or talk to anyone, but you try to spot your loved ones as you enter, and you know they are anxiously looking for you, but not a sound can be uttered.

One person after the next we are called and asked a particular question. I remember thinking to myself, 'I hope they don't say anything stupid to make the judge mad before I get up there'. After what seemed like forever, my name was called. When asked if there were any family or friends that wanted to stand with me, my mother came up and to my surprise, the pastor and his wife from Charleston had come to support me. I had met with them several times for counseling. I kept in touch with them by writing when I was in Lexington County and they always responded.

Here we go; the probation department had stated their case. And it was ugly but it was indeed all true. He asked to hear from my mother, then the Pastors and then he asked was there anything I would like to share. I asked if I could read a letter I had written to them and he approved. I read it and don't even remember reading it. I know now that it was Holy Spirit carrying me through. The judge thanked me for being so honest and then he gave me my sentence. I honestly don't remember hearing anything but 5 years and I was satisfied with that, considering I was looking at 10, and my track record didn't look very good. As they sat me back down and finished up with the rest of the inmates, I was called into a room to sign all my paperwork. This is when I was explained my sentence. The judge sentenced me to 5 years' probation but asked back for the time I was on the run which was 18 months. Meaning he wanted me to do this part back at the South Carolina Department of Corrections, then I would do the rest on probation. When I understood what he had given me, my heart was smiling. Although I had to go back to prison for the second time, it could have been a lot worse, so this was ok with me. Plus I knew I had prayed for God's will and this must have been it. When my mother came to visit me that week, she was telling me about court. I was there but I did not remember much at all. She said when I read my letter that everyone's mouth was wide open and that it was so silent you couldn't hear a pin drop. She said everyone was captivated by the sincerity of my heart when I read my letter.

I know Holy Spirit had me write the letter and had me share it; therefore it had to be received with love.

I have been in a prison all my life and now I am on my way back to prison behind bars again but this time it is where the bars that have been placed on my life are finally starting to come down once and for all.

It doesn't take long for them to come and get you from county jail to State prison, but boy is that transition challenging and humiliating. I tried not to concentrate on the negative because I KNEW in my HEART OF HEARTS that this would be the VERY LAST time I would EVER have to go through this ever again. R & E (reception and evaluation) holding is the worst part. It's testing you for everything medically, classifying you and making sure you go to the right compound. The hardest part is you are locked in a room 23 hours a day, its freezing, and you have to do everything from a slot in your door. I chose to read my bible, write a lot and make the BEST of it. I CHOSE TO HAVE JOY

UNSPEAKABLE and let NOTHING get me down!!!!! After they told me the compound I would go to, I was relieved. Although it was the same one I was in the first time and it would be embarrassing to go back; knowing there would be people there that had longer sentences than I had when I went in first time, but I had to hold it together and let go of my pride. This was about me getting and keeping myself humble before the Lord and transforming into who He has called me to be. I was just thankful to be alive and be free even if I was behind bars.

Heather A. Cook

CLOTHED IN RIGHTEOUSNESS
CHAPTER EIGHT

This is where my new life began. All the old things had passed away and all things became new. Some may be asking, "How is that possible? Look at where you are." Family, this is where God changed my name. In my transparency, I learned how to be transformed by changing my thinking. Yes it was where for the very first time, I learned how to live.

You see, it's easy not to make a commitment to change while in prison. Jail could be an institution for rehabilitation, but for the most part it is not. Jail is like the similitude of a parent and child relative to the "TIME-OUT." system. This is supposed to silence the child enough for him to think about his actions, hoping the lesson would be learned and there would not be a repeat offense. Only some children will get it the first time. Confinement is not favorable, so to avoid chastisement or punishment he will not repeat the behavior. On the other side of reason, when this child goes to confinement, he uses his time to think of ways to escape punishment. So he comes up with a different strategy of how NOT to get caught.

There are people who are jailed for criminal activity.

They come in a criminal but leave a better criminal. In this system there are destructive things you could choose to get involved with such as…

- Drugs
- Lies
- Hustling
- Same sex relationships
- Stealing
- Gangs

The list goes on and on, or you can choose change for the better. I decided to change for the better. I got involved with anything positive, making the best out of my days and doing everything to the Glory of God. The compound is a work release program. My job was ground maintenance again. There were acres and acres of yard to manicure and it didn't matter if it were a hundred degree weather or 20 below 0, we were still held to the standard of completion. I reminisce pushing that lawnmower; thanking God for how wonderful He is. I would lift my hands up every moment I got. The other ladies would ask me, "How do you stay so happy all the time?" That was the perfect time for me to plug them into Jesus, so I took the opportunity to tell them how incredibly awesome He is.

Remember those slips of paper I used to write scriptures on in the county jail, well every morning before work I would pass them out to those I worked with. After a while there were others that would come up to me and ask me for one and others that would ask me to pray with them or for them.

The Holy Spirit prompted me to make myself available to the women coming into the work release program. I started a Bible study and worship services, It was hard to find anyone who proclaimed Jesus Christ as Lord, but I continued to search. Then the Lord showed me the right candidate. Her name is Sissy Sanders. She had a sentence of 20 years and been incarcerated for 13 of those years when we met. There was something special and different about Sissy. We started a friendship and built a strong sister bond. Sissy and I encouraged each other every day. We spent time in the yard praying and having Bible study. God gave me Sissy for sure and for that, I am thankful.

There were several women I wrote from the Christian groups that came to minister. I just want to keep in contact with them for accountability and so they would not forget me. There was a woman in a group called the God Squad. Her name is Karen Alexander. When she told her testimony, I knew she would be one God showed me. I wrote her about once a week just to let her know who I am and what were some issues, challenges, and hang-ups I dealt with. Moreover, if she could help me identify some behaviors, I would be grateful. As of now, we still have a standing relationship and still keep in contact with each other.

Shekinah Glory Church came in once a week for Bible study. They really touched my heart. It was in one of their services I received the filling of the Holy Spirit with speaking with tongues. I remember this so well. I had heard others speak with tongues and wanted it; not understanding what it meant fully. I just knew if God was giving it as a gift, I wanted it. After Bible study one night, we were praying out and as I started to pray, the Holy Spirit gave me utterance; and there it was I was speaking and praying in an unknown tongue. I'm so thankful especially knowing why it's important. The Holy Spirit is what sustained me then and continues to sustain me now. Today I am in contact with them and we've been involved with an evangelistic ministry called *Time to Revive.*

The ladies from God's Church of Deliverance came once a week. Sherry Lewis and Karine Daymon stood out in this group. This entire group really blessed me. There were truly something sweet and real about them and when it came time for me to leave, I knew that I would need to stay in touch with them. God made it possible for that to happen, after leaving I found out that Sherry lived moments from my mother's house.

While in prison I made plans to move back in with my mother and children. I recalled the Holy Spirit warning me that I would experience discord to a greater magnitude than what I experienced previously when I lived with my Mother. However, I was not allowed to leave her house until released by the Holy Spirit. I had to war in the spirit concerning these matters because the relationship between my mother and me was very unhealthy. The spirit in my mother came against me all the time and it was really hard cohabiting together. There were days when I just wanted to leave. I didn't want to work it out because of the pain, the hurt and the distrust on each of our part. When I sense I was losing sight on what God had spoken, I would call Sherry and she would help me through by praying and constantly reminding me it was not time to go. There were times my mother would put all my belongings out by the road and tell me to leave. My oldest son and I would gather it and bring it all back in the house time after time. I'm sure it's looking like I was bucking authority, but I had to say to her, "I'm not going anywhere until the Lord says so." All I wanted was by the help of the Holy Spirit to get it right as a mother, as a daughter and to put my shattered life back together. This was the greatest opportunity to practice the love and forgiveness I learned through the Scriptures and spiritual-help books. I learned acceptance and how to fight in the spirit and not the flesh. I was determined to win, so I stayed. After six months of being out of the system, I was able to save some money. I got the release from Holy Spirit so I moved out from my mother and took Jared and Kennedy with me. Darius wanted to stay with his grandmother.

Moving out was amazing. The Lord provided for us time after time. I thank God for Sherry because she, like an angel was there for us the whole time. She came everyday if there was a Bible study or worship service, or just for us all to hang out with her family. She made sacrifices that my children and I could never repay. The only payment I have is to continually walk with the Lord. She has taught me so much about being a true woman of God. She loved me enough to show me the way and to correct me when I was wrong. I am forever grateful for her being in my life.

Our friendship got my children and I connected to a blessed congregation called God's Church of Deliverance with Bishop Milton and Mattie Mosby. This is where I learned about God's word from Genesis to Revelation and about the Holy Spirit. My praise and worship was uninhibited and free but to be in a place where I was received by my worship and praise was just liberating. God has delivered me from the bondage of my past. I will always show my exuberant joy. Bishop Mosby is a true shepherd of God's Kingdom and I am truly thankful for his life.

Through him, God showed me some of my gifts. Bishop Mosby gave me freedom to worship, to work with the children in Sunday school, and on the praise dance team. His love is genuine, as he is a praying pastor. He was always in tune with the Holy Spirit. I never could go to him and tell him something that would shock him because as he prayed, Holy Spirit would reveal to him or give him a word of knowledge concerning me. I'm grateful to have him as a father in The Lord.

CARRIER OF HIS PRESENCE
CHAPTER NINE

God is now alive in me and through me and I want Him to remain strong so I can survive. With a solid resolve and determination, GREAT will be my reward. I had a blessed assurance NOTHING could stop.

In retrospect, I was on probation for over 15 years. Year after year the shadow of my dreadful past was attached to me like a ball and chain. I would do well for a while however my discipline was only strong and fierce for my demonic cravings, so I'd fall off the wagon in a vicious cycle of addiction and bondage. I remember the faces when I returned to jail or the probation office after being caught or back to the streets, and they would shake their heads about me, and what this said to me was how worthless I was. This reminds me of a quote by Fannie Hamer, "I'm sick and tired of being sick and tired." But I could really identify with this quote, "My sickness is sick of me."

There were these two ladies at the probation department that offered guidance, support and some kind of hope, but it was never the kind I understood, it was just words that sounded good and worked for me only a minute. Finally, I finished probation early and for the VERY FIRST TIME I HAD NO PAPERS FOLLOWING ME. I was really free. I am so glad that King Jesus never looked at me the way judgmental people did; because GOD KNEW MY WORTH.

Next I needed to get my license back but had so many fines and fees to pay before I could even take my DUI class. I didn't have the financial means available to make it all happen, but God gave me a friend who believed in me and prayed for me through the years. They made a sacrifice to pay all my fines so I could get my driving privileges back. After the fines and fees were satisfied, In order to get my driver's license back, I had to take the driving test again. I haven't had that kind of privilege since the first time I got my license, when I was sixteen. I give glory to God for making a way for me.

My dad knew I couldn't afford a car so he purchased a van from his wife's family. The vehicle belonged to her late father and I was so thankful. My dad supported me in hopes believing in me that I would do the right thing. He confirmed by his act of love that he trusted me to stay on the straight and narrow this time. I took the test in the van my dad

> He confirmed by his act of love that he trusted me to stay on the straight and narrow this time.

purchased for me and passed it on the first try.

Time after time God showed me how mighty He is. Two of my boys lived with me, one of which I lost all rights to. My mother adopted him so that allowed me opportunity to be his parent again and I was so happy we had our own place; a place for my other children to stay when they visited, and a place we could finally call home.

After a year in our apartment, I needed to get Logan back with us. She was having issues with Travis' cousin, but further than that it was just time. The boys and I periodically discussed having Logan live with us. We all wanted her there, but our space seemed limited. The Holy Spirit however was tugging on my heart to search on what it would take. I'd been told I lost custody of Logan and with my head so messed up over the years; I couldn't decipher what was true.

So I began to search it out. I went to the courthouse where I found there were no papers filed with the clerk of courts. The courthouse suggested I should check with DSS (Department of Social Services). Following up that lead, there showed no paper work there either. A DSS official said, "There is nothing keeping you from getting your child; go get her." "What?" As wonderful and exciting as that sounded a burst of fear came over me! I thought about what my oldest son said, "Mom, how will Logan live with us? We only have two bedrooms and one bathroom." I felt stuck between a rock and hard place; not knowing what to do. The good news of Logan being with us was both thrilling and paralyzing. Over and over his voice repeated in my mind, "How will this work?"

DSS told me this on a Friday and Logan was trying to figure out why I had not come for her. When the sun rose up on Monday, I sat on the edge of my bed pondering what to do next. I opened up my notebook and my eyes fell on this passage, "Without faith it is impossible to please God." Right then, I knew she was coming home.

I asked Logan's grandmother to meet me because I felt that it might not go well so she met me at the Cracker barrel down the road from where Logan lived. When we left to get Logan this song was playing on the radio, "TAKE BACK WHAT THE DEVIL STOLE FROM YOU." That piece of encouragement was all God! Now I have three of my kids all under the same roof; all together with me. Truly only the Lord could restore us back together again. What a perfect picture of God's restoration. His love continually blows me away.

In prison I was on the praise dance team. Gail Faust came in to teach us once a week. She was a minister of dance and she was amazing. I told her when I got out; I'd be looking her up. She owned Columbia

Community Arts Center formally Ly-Ben Christian Dance Theatre. Finding her in the phone book was a blissful moment especially telling her who I was. As we made connection she offered me a part time position at the front desk. She played a huge part on how God worked all things for my good and His Glory. I thought to myself, 'Lord this could only be You.' I'm right out of prison and already have a job never being rejected. Of course my answer was YES as loud as it could be. I was filled with gratitude and thanksgiving.

I stood to learn more maturing as a person and a woman of God but I was thankful for what God allowed Mrs. Gail to do for me. There were things I had taken for granted, but thankfully, Mrs. Gail and I are still friends. Not a day goes by without reflections of how blessed I am. She gave me the opportunity most would not have. God used her to help and bless me in more ways than one.

I am so appreciative for every door that opened for me from then on out. I worked for a Christian International School called World Life Education. We helped children from Africa to get their Scholastic Aptitude Test (SAT), and Test of English as a Foreign Language (TOEFL) exams accomplished, to get booked with the Embassy and searched for them to be accepted into colleges here in the US. I was able to meet so many wonderful people.

After that I met a wonderful man of God, Pastor John Lastinger of New Covenant Church. We met at a prayer breakfast I attended once a month called City Light. He approached me to reach out to one of his church members and from there I started working as an administrator at the church. The church had a home on the property and no one was living in it. It was a very large house with 4 bedrooms and 3 full bathrooms, living room, dining room and kitchen. Plenty of room for all of us without us having to share a room or be on top of each other. The house needed some renovations, but the Pastor said we could move in. On Sundays, he took offerings to pay for supplies. It didn't take long to complete the renovations. Afterwards, we were able to move in. What a blessing he, his family and the church became to my family and me.

November 2012, I was invited to a youth celebration by a sister of mine. I brought the youth department from God's Church of Deliverance. We were ushered to the first row next to my best friend Jami on one side and a gentleman covered in mime face paint on the other side. He was there to minister in dance. I asked his name and he told me Willie. As the night went on, our row was in praise & worship. I had taken a lot of pictures and before Willie left I gave him my email address. I'd plan to upload them on Facebook and tag him. He found me on Facebook and we started chatting in Messenger. After a couple of weeks chatting with each other, he made a random post that he was on 24 hour staff duty and wanted a meal from McDonalds, naming the number of the meal. I asked my oldest son to take a ride with me. I purchased his food and sent him a message I had his food but didn't know where to bring it. He couldn't believe we had his food and were trying to get it to him. He gave us directions to the building. This was the first time we saw each other since the youth conference. This made the start of something wonderful.

In 2013 after several months of hanging out together, we decided to date. Willie let me know his affections by writing on my bathroom mirror with soap, "I Love You Heather Pounds." What a Valentine's Day card. I knew Willie would be leaving for Korea that May, but I was not moved by it. I knew this was going to be a long lasting relationship. About two weeks before Willie is due to leave for Korea, he ministered in dance at Pastor John's church to a song called "Yes." It was amazingly awesome. I love seeing him operating under the influence of Holy Spirit. His friends came to see him before he was to leave the country.

After the service Pastor John asked Willie to close out in prayer. As he was praying, he asked me to marry him. It took me a minute to catch up with what just happened. Did I just hear correctly? I couldn't believe he just asked me to marry him but when it registered I responded with a resounding YES; showing my uninhibited joy, sprinting around the church.

It was like a fairy tale. Is this really true? Somebody pinch me! We decided to set a date having only two weeks to plan. Mrs. Robbie and the ladies from New Covenant offered to plan my wedding and all that was needed was $40 and my colors. Everything looked so amazing. Willie's best friend, Creshawna my new sister-in-law bought my wedding gown and everything was perfect and on April 28 2013, Pastor John married Willie and me. Willie left in a few weeks for one year. It was truly by the grace, mercy and strength of the Lord that brought us through.

I'm very thankful for my husband taking on a huge responsibility for a family of six; a woman with five children of which none are his biologically. We are constantly coming together as one big family. God's love continues to push us forward. God has been so very good to me.

I'm so thankful for the many opportunities I've had to let my light shine in Christ. I've gone into high schools to share with students the importance of making good decisions. I was part of a program called the Richland County READY Program where troubled kids stayed overnight at the court house in a cell and I could share my story with them. I've talked with the kids in DJJ (Department of Juvenile Justice).

I've shared with the ladies in the prison where I was incarcerated. That was truly an experience because here I am in regular clothes looking at ladies who are wearing the same jumpsuit I used to wear. Now I'm standing in the same place I once stood and I testify of God's grace and mercy. I've seen several women from the streets inside; some with longer sentences than me. His mercy endures forever.

I was involved in a ministry called PIC Positive Images Consulting. We did Empowerment once a month. We had a different topic every month and shared on it then opened the floor for others who attended to share or ask questions.

I am currently involved with a worldwide ministry called *Time to Revive* based out of Dallas Texas; Dr. Kyle Lance Martin is the founder. This is an Evangelistic ministry that is invited to different states for revival. I began with them when they came to my home town for Revive Columbia and that's when I jumped on board. They bring churches together; train, teach and equip people to share the Gospel of Jesus Christ; this is what I love to do most. I've been to

Minnesota for Revive TWIN CITIES and Indiana for 196 days of Revival in Indiana. We started with seven days of prayer and ended up 52 days in Elkhart /Goshen area as revival fire broke out. As the fire continued to spread the 196th day ended in a celebration where over 6000 believers and followers of Christ of all denominations, gathered together to worship and praise God for what was taking place. There were 2,576 salvations recorded and discipleship makers in place for all of them. It truly has been a high time in the Lord. I am also involved with Mississippi for Revive Tupelo. It doesn't stop there because wherever the next stops are I will join them there also.

I have met lots of women through Time to Revive by going into different areas of my hometown in Revive Columbia SC. These women just want to find hope and love. The Holy Spirit gave me an idea of bringing the women together a couple times a month for fellowship and discipleship. We gathered at a local restaurant for dinner and fellowship while the kids enjoyed play. It wasn't long before the group grew larger so we moved to a new fellowship area. I was home one day spending time with Daddy God and He gave me a vision of an emerald. As I thought of the emerald I envisioned each face of the ladies in the group. While thanking God for bringing each one in my life, the Holy Spirit spoke to me saying, "Heather, you are all Emeralds of my Grace." The tears began to roll down my face. That moment our Chic-Fil-A group had a name change. We are now the "EMERALDS OF GRACE." As I shared this with the ladies, they loved the name and it put new meaning on things and gave us all something to look forward to.

From the beginning of this book, you have journeyed through quite a few of the jail sentences handed to me; to include self-imprisonment of my mind, dead places in my soul and a resurrected spirit. The bars opened, the chains fell off and this one woman experiences on a daily basis TRUE FREEDOM!

My children are blessed and I'm blessed to have them. They were all dealt a hand that could've broken them; however they chose to rise above the broken places. I am so thankful for how God kept my children and Mother through all they experienced. My Mother endured my failures and gave compassion to her grandchildren.

> The bars opened, the chains fell off and this one woman experiences on a daily basis TRUE FREEDOM!

God has a perfect plan for us and that makes life worth living. Marrying my husband has been a blessing to our whole family. Willie fights for his country as a US Army Soldier for our freedom. Europe (Germany) will be our home for a time. It blows my mind when I look at where I was and where I am now; only God can do this! I was never to leave the states for half my life, but now I live in another country and it's all legal. It just shows that when God is for you who can be against you. God is the final authority and He has the FINAL say so.

My life would be nothing if it weren't for the blood of Jesus Christ and my decision to make Jesus Lord of my life. It won't always be easy but the rewards are always worth it. I overcome by the blood of the Lamb and the words of my testimony. God gave me everything so I have a responsibility to give God everything I have.

Consider your life not being your own, but rather consider to whom your life belongs. When I figured that out, that's when things started to turn around for me. This is a process of transformation and as long as I stay in Christ's will, He is able, willing, and ready to help and bless me. Every day I am able to see more and more of the old me fall away.

> God gave me everything so I have a responsibility to give God everything I have.

I am able to see where the prison bars unlocked and I walked out into a new life filled with joy, hope and love.

I have to press! I have to pull! I have to push my way through because the rewards are always worth it. Jesus is a stain remover, a sustainer, and a life giver. Without Him I would fail but with Him I always win. There's been lots of damage done to me and by me, but Jesus has delivered me from it all. Step by step, day by day He has given me peace, joy and love. His Word and Promises are available. You can stand on it. My friends, that's all we need. Period!

Jesus took a messed up, throw away, damaged little girl like me and gave me beauty for my ashes, joy for my sadness and a garment of praise for my heaviness.

This is this woman's journey to true freedom. Come join me!

May God bless each one of you who have read this book and have sown into my life.

Coming soon a new title, **Damaged but Delivered, Healing from the Inside Out**

Love covers all,

Heather Cook

MORE ABOUT THE AUTHOR

Heather Ann Cook - 1976 was born Heather Ann Pounds in a rural town outside of Columbia SC.

Heather is a mother of 5 children and the wife of Willie Cook a United States Military soldier. They reside in Kaiserslautern, Germany.

She is a homemaker and this allows her to serve others as she serves our Lord and Savior, Jesus Christ. She and her husband have opened their home in Germany to minister to others through Coffee, Canvases & Conversations. Heather is often found traveling with an Evangelistic ministry called *Time to Revive*.

Heather is a person who expresses the joy of The Lord and love for others. She believes true freedom only comes when people receive Jesus Christ as their Savior and their Lord. Her heart's passion is to travel around the world meeting others and making an imprint on their lives.

Heather is excited to become a new author with her first book **Beyond the Bars, One Woman's Journey to TRUE FREEDOM**. Her prayer is that this book be used as a testimony of God's grace, mercies and unfailing love towards each one of us. For those who read it with struggles themselves or have a loved one who struggles, that their hope will be discovered at the Cross.

Heather asks if you have never received Jesus Christ as your Savior and your Lord would you please read the following scriptures.

Romans 3:23 for we all sin and fall short of the glory of God.

Romans 6:23 for the wages of sin is death, but the gift of God is eternal life in Jesus our Lord.

Romans 5:8 But God demonstrates His own love towards us, in while we were still yet sinners, Christ died for us

Ephesians 2:8-9 for by grace you have been saved through faith; and not of yourselves, it is a gift of God not as a result of works, so that no one may boast

Romans 10:9-10 that if you confess with your mouth Jesus as Lord, and believe in your heart that God raised Him from the dead, you will be saved. For with the heart a person believes, resulting in righteousness, and with the mouth he confesses, resulting in Salvation

If you have read these and say yes to Jesus Christ there are angels in heaven rejoicing and so are we. Please contact us at www.kingdombuilderspublications.com and let us know.

Love covers all,

Heather Cook

Jami Salters posted on her Facebook page,...

Help me by describing in your own words
if you have ever seen or had the pleasure to meet Heather
Cook, what stands out to you OR what would you remember
her by:

Ke Ke Colbert: *Her presence...*
She has the glory of the Lord shining on, in and through her!

LeTasha S. Robinson: *One that truly has a heart to*
worship and praise God regardless of how it looks. My spirit
picks up an authentic praise and worship when I'm around her.

Brigit "QueenBee." Malloy: *Her undignified praise!!!!!!*
Yes God!!!!

Vickie Crout Rinehart: *Her excitements while praising,*
her bright smile and personality, her beauty, inside and out!

Angela Armstrong: *I only met her through Facebook &*
she is married to my nephew, I love her zeal for the Lord. Her
enthusiasm for knowing God has her Lord and Savior flowing
all over the page.

Nancy Brown Scruggs: *There is a light that shines*
through her, a light that surrounds her and that light is the
Holy Spirit.

Toni McMickin Smith: *I met her through Willie. I can*
say the spirit of the Lord shines in her so much it reflects on you
if you're standing near her. It's very obvious how much she loves
him.

Debra Comstock Hammer: *Raw honesty, sincere spirituality and refreshingly hopeful. I met her through a women's ministry overseas.*

Sherian D: Foster *Simply amazing*

Colleen Jenkins: *I met her at Revive Indiana. I watched her dance and fell in love with her grace and beauty. She is truly a Warrior Princess for God's kingdom.*

Valerie Lever: *When I think of Heather I think of a wild child headed down the wrong roads of life and after years of being lost God showed her the way....so I would say WILD CHILD to GOD CHILD*

Gloria Miller: *Exuberant passion for her LORD JESUS CHRIST and the desire that everyone would experience the same!!!*

Lisa Mills: *Contagious joy!*

Angie Sarah Schultz: *Heather is on fire with our Lord.... That fire gets under her feet making her gracefully dance around like a Mexican jumping bean...... always has a smile and loving words flowing from her*

Jane Rae LaDue: *Always beaming with a smile and happy.*

Holly Armstrong: *I have never met her in person, she has taken the time for me to pray and write to me and I adore her! She has been redeemed and transformed and lives Jesus. She is using His love and her testimony to reach out and is saving the* *lost. I found her on here and I am not letting her go and can't wait for the book, we have a lot in common.*

Dioncia Wells: *Cannon her praise, worship and love for God, family and friends*

Karen Watts: *Heather's contagious joy in worship and genuine love for everyone she meets has deeply impacted me!*

Pineda Hector Laurie: *FRONTLINE WARRIOR!*

Alysha Homewood: *When I see Heather Cook I just seem complete freedom, and a uncontainable joy. I see hope and love! Which we can thank god! She is a living testimony. That shines sooo bright*

Martha Hedtke: *I met Heather Cook when I picked her up at the airport for Revive Twin Cities. She loves the Lord with all her heart and shares this love openly with all she meets. I love her, too!!!*

Nicole Lincourt: *Her positive outlook on life; her love and devotion to our Heavenly Father and her family. Heather Cook is by far an amazing woman of God who I am blessed to know!*

Deborah Pate: *Although I have never met Heather in person, I would have to say, encouraging, just by being real. Uplifting, prayer warrior, a child of the Almighty God, who uses Grace to minister to others!! And a Blessing to those lives she comes in contact with, including mine!!*

Shaniqua Lewis: *Knowing Heather has been a blessing to me and my kids. No matter what she was going through she was always happy and looking at the bright side of things. I* *just love the woman she has allowed the world to see, the woman she has always been. I love you Heather Cook*

Karen Ron Alexander: *I met Heather Cook thru SCDC. I met a woman who came into the system a tired, angry at the world woman who had questions about God and her life. One who would come up to the altar and pray crying out to God about her life and shame.*

Kimberly Howard: *Heather Cook: Pure radiant light shines from her....you can't help notice her because Jesus is alive and well in her! Pure joy is heard in her voice and movements. If you've never met her, you're missing The Holy Spirit wrapped in an earthen vessel and if you've been blessed to meet her, you'll never be the same.*

Angela Jackson: *Sister of Worship unto our God, her smile and her zeal to bring all to Jesus Christ.*

Kay Pittman: *I met Heather Cook after she surrendered her life to Jesus Christ. She is a precious sister in Christ with enough "fire" in her faith to light the faith of another! Her joy is so contagious and her faith shines like a diamond! You are loved Heather Cook*

Dora Schmucker: *Her energy and without a doubt love for her savior Jesus Christ.*

Miriam A. Murtaugh: *Lover of Jesus...and I don't mean that in the empty, over-used, religious sense of the term. I mean one who has "been with Yeshua." One who has shared intimacy with HIM, which cannot be expressed with words, yet it glows in her countenance and changes the atmosphere where* *she walks because she carries HIM in her DNA. His love resonates in Heather....*

Rolly Slaubaugh: *The bubbly joy, very passionate about her love for Jesus, and her deep desire for others to find freedom!! She is like twice freed and knows it!!!!!!!*

Briana Slaubaugh: *A beautiful example of a true believer; with a love and passion for Jesus and for others.*

Angela Kilgo Mallon: *Always uplifting, desires to keep the Love and communication with Christ our Lord.*

Doug Stukes: *Heather is a survivor, an overcomer who has challenged herself to break the barriers set against her... Her self-determination and willingness to submit to her God is motivation to all who know her... The freedom we have witnessed from her praise and dance comes from a sincerely humble heart... Heather is an example of God dwelling on the inside of a person...*

Denise Henke: *JOY OVERFLOWING!*

Sandra Kovacs: *Her smile!*

Stephanie Hayes *I have only been blessed to spend a little time with her so far. But in that small window of time she impacted my thoughts about true worship and she has such a joy about her even when she talks about her past. Can't wait till that time when I get to spend more time with Heather Cook. She is truly an on fire God Chaser!!*

Whitney McWhorter: *Heather is life. She is a spark that quickly boils into a fire and it's contagious.*

Beyond the Bars

Michelle McIlravy: *I remember watching heather worship in Columbia SC and it stirred something deep within me!! Un-abandoned joy and complete freedom in Christ*

Melissa Exline: *A real example of how God can truly transform one and turn ashes to beauty! What I see in Heather is how to love unconditionally!!*

Susie Harmon Hartley: *Genuine, when I see Heather I think of He, who has been forgiven much, loves much!! She's like Mary Madeline!! Love her to the moon and back!!*

Movita Bovain: *Heather Cook loves to stand on Holy ground literally took her shoes off everywhere!!!!!!*

JesseandMichelle Loera: *She has a special gift of making everyone she meets feel like the most important and most loved individual on Earth!*

Lane Bass: *I first met Heather in a home worship gathering. I see an all-out worshipper, one with whom the enemy just scratches his head, wondering what to do. One whose worship is a direct blow to the religious spirit*

Summer Patterson: *The first and only time I saw/met Heather was in MS at the Gathering.. She was in a white dress and worshipped God in a way I wanted to so badly.. She stood out in the room and had magnificent flags she danced with. My 4 year old daughter watched her until she couldn't stand it anymore and ran up, grabbed one of Heather's spare flags and followed her every move. Heather; not knowing me or my child never thought twice of her to using the flag and dancing* *with her. I have never heard her preach, never heard her testimony and knew nothing about her except from what I saw. And what I saw was a true relationship with God, some ppl covet and others are too worried about 'self' to even get to that level with Him!*

Angela Adams: *Her faith; no matter what life throws at her, she still trusts the Lord.*

Melodie A. Phillips: *Princess Warrior with determination to seek God & put Him first in every situation! Praises with all her heart, soul & spirit; She is such an inspiration.*

KayWill Wilson: *ONE word: JOYFUL!*

Renée Davis: *I love watching Heather worship. It is very evident that she loves the Lord with her whole mind, body, and soul.*

Erin Graber Miller: *A woman transformed by Jesus and radiates His love in everything she does!*

Bonnie Balogh Rosado: *Joyful overcomer.*

CPSIA information can be obtained
at www.ICGtesting.com
Printed in the USA
FFHW010952020219
50334980-55405FF